The SNOW PRINCESS
COOKBOOK

BARBARA BEERY

FAMILIUS

Published by Familius LLC, www.familius.com

Familius books are available at special discounts for bulk purchases for sales promotions, family
or corporate use. Special editions, including personalized covers, excerpts of existing books,
or books with corporate logos, can be created in large quantities for special needs. For more
information, contact Premium Sales at 559-876-2170 or email specialmarkets@familius.com.

Library of Congress Catalog-in-Publication Data
2015931056   ISBN 9781939629753

Photography by Lisette Donado and Greer Inez
Cover and book design by David Miles

10 9 8 7 6 5 4 3 2 1

First Edition

Printed in China

CONTENTS

SIPPING TREATS

PARTY CRAFTS

DIETARY GUIDE

- **GF** GLUTEN FREE
- **Veg** VEGETARIAN
- **V** VEGAN
- **DF** DAIRY FREE

Dear Parents,

I've worked with thousands of kids and parents over the years at our Foodie Kids culinary center, and I know that accommodating allergies and dietary needs can sometimes be challenging. We've done our best to make things easy in this book by clearly identifying which recipes are gluten free, vegetarian, vegan, and/or dairy free. But for those that aren't marked, remember that you can easily swap out ingredients (almond milk for regular milk, gluten-free flour for all-purpose flour, and so on) to make the recipes work for your child. Hope you enjoy!

—*Barbara Beery*

FROZEN TREATS

"YOU SNOW GIRL" BANANA POPS

1 Trim one end of each banana to create a flat surface.

2 Lightly brush or spray orange juice on each banana to keep it from turning brown.

3 Insert a decorative paper straw or Popsicle® stick into each banana, and allow them to dry on a platter for 5 minutes prior to decorating.

4 Using a bit of frosting or piping gel, adhere facial features to each banana.

5 Secure the sugar eyes and create eyelashes with black fondant. Draw the mouth with pink or red fondant and the nose with orange fondant.

6 Insert pretzel sticks for arms and create little hands with black fondant. Insert several noodles into the top of each banana for hair and adorn with a colorful ribbon.

Veg

INGREDIENTS

....

Bananas, peeled (1 per person)

1 orange, juiced

Decorative paper straws or Popsicle® sticks

Black frosting or piping gel

Sugar eyes*

Colored fondants (black, pink or red, and orange)**

Pretzel sticks***

Cellophane or rice noodles, broken into 2-inch pieces

Packaged vanilla frosting or piping gel

Colorful ribbon

MAKES AS MANY AS NEEDED

7 Place the bananas on a tray and cover with plastic wrap. Store in the refrigerator until ready to use.

8 Banana Pops must be eaten the same day they are made.

* Sugar eyes and fondants may be purchased at Michael's craft stores or online at amazon.com.

** The packaged colored fondants are made by CK Products. Wilton and Fondarific are our favorite brands! Check them out at: http://www.wilton.com/ and http://fondarific.com/.

GF **** Substitute with gluten-free pretzel sticks, if desired.*

SNOW MOUNTAIN FROZEN YOGURT

WITH MARSHMALLOW CREAM

1 Mix together the Greek yogurt, honey, lemon juice, and vanilla extract and refrigerate for 1 hour.

2 Pour the mixture into an ice cream maker and process according to the manufacturer's instructions.

3 Remove from the machine and place in a covered container in the freezer until ready to use.

4 Serve with marshmallow cream, and garnish with snowflake sprinkles and mini marshmallows or fresh fruits of your choice.

DF *Substitute with soy or coconut yogurt for a dairy-free option.*

INGREDIENTS

· · · · · · · · · · · · · · · · · ·

3 cups plain whole milk Greek yogurt*

1/2 cup honey, agave, or pure maple syrup

2 teaspoons fresh lemon juice

1 teaspoon pure vanilla extract

Ice cream maker

Marshmallow Cream (see page 11)

Snowflake sprinkles and mini marshmallows

Fresh fruit (optional)

MAKES 5–6 CUPS

MARSHMALLOW CREAM

1 In a large bowl, combine egg whites, corn syrup, and salt; beat with an electric mixer on high for 10 minutes, or until thick.

2 Add powdered sugar; beat on low until blended. Beat in vanilla and food coloring.

3 Store covered in the refrigerator for up to 2 days.

As an alternative, purchase marshmallow cream and stir in food coloring, if desired.

* Paste food colorings produce the truest colors for any frosting. They are made by both Wilton and AmeriColor and may be found online or in Michael's or JoAnn craft stores.

Looking for an all-natural coloring alternative? Foodie Kids loves these two companies for all natural food colorings: India Tree and Maggie's Naturals. For more information, check out Maggie's Naturals (a very heart-warming store behind this line) at http://www.maggiesnaturals.com/ and India Tree at http://www.indiatree.com/Category_Page.php?Category=NC.

GF **DF** **Veg**

INGREDIENTS

. . . .

3 egg whites

2 cups light corn syrup

1/2 teaspoon sea salt

2 cups powdered sugar

1 tablespoon pure vanilla extract

Blue paste food coloring*

MAKES 3 CUPS

SPARKLING ICE SNOW CONES

GF **DF** **V**

INGREDIENTS

. . . .

Blue Curacao Syrup* (about 1–2 teaspoons per person)

Squeeze-top bottle

Snow cone maker or food processor

Ice cubes of any shape your freezer makes

SERVES AS MANY AS NEEDED

1 Place desired amount of syrup into a squeeze top bottle.

2 Crush ice in a snow cone maker or food processor.

3 Fill your container of choice with shaved ice and drizzle with syrup.

4 Serve as soon as possible!

* We like Monin non-alcoholic syrup.

SNOW PRINCESS SERVING SUGGESTION: *Try using other flavors and colors of pre-made syrups. Many are available with organic fruits and natural food dyes, such as Nature's Flavors at http://naturesflavors.com/syrups/organic-flavor-syrups/organic-snow-cone-syrups.*

FROZEN HEART ICE CREAM SANDWICHES

INGREDIENTS

....

1/2 cup butter, softened

3/4 cup granulated sugar or coconut sugar

1 egg

1 teaspoon pure vanilla

2 cups flour**

1/2 teaspoon baking soda

1/4 teaspoon sea salt

Medium and small heart-shaped cookie cutters

Vanilla Buttercream Frosting (page 18)

Blue decorating sugar

Frozen vanilla yogurt or ice cream, slightly softened

MAKES 24 COOKIES

1 Preheat oven to 375 degrees. Line two sheet pans with parchment paper; set aside until ready to use.

2 Cream butter in a large mixing bowl: Combine butter with sugar, beating until light and fluffy. Add egg and vanilla, mixing well.

3 Combine flour, soda, and salt in a separate bowl and add to creamed mixture, blending well. The dough will be very stiff. Roll it approximately 1/4-inch thick on a lightly floured work area.

4 Cut out dough with a medium heart-shaped cookie cutter. For half of the cookies, cut out a tiny heart with the smaller heart-shaped cookie cutter.

5 Bake for 8–10 minutes, or until lightly browned. Remove from the oven and place on wire racks to cool completely before decorating.

6 Frost the cookies with the cut-out heart centers and sprinkle with blue decorating sugar. Shake off excess sugar.

7 Place about 1 tablespoon of slightly softened frozen yogurt or ice cream on top of each undecorated heart cookie and top with a frosted and decorated heart cookie.

8 Store ice cream sandwiches in the freezer until ready to use (at least 3 hours prior to serving), or store for up to one week.

SNOW PRINCESS FUN IDEA! *Frost and decorate each tiny heart cut-out as an extra little cookie treat to serve with the ice cream sandwiches.*

* Substitute with your favorite packaged sugar cookies or cookie dough. Please note that packaged cookie dough will not have the same texture and may be more difficult to cut out.

GF *** Substitute with gluten-free flour and adapt measurements according to package directions.*

DIPPITY-DOO-DAH PARTY CONE CUPCAKES

1 Line two cookie sheets with parchment paper; set aside until ready to use.

2 Melt candy coating according to package directions. Place in a shallow dish and dip the pointed end of each cone into the coating. Place each cone on the prepared sheet pan and set in the refrigerator until hardened, at least 10 minutes, or up to 24 hours.

3 Frost and decorate the cupcakes with homemade Vanilla Buttercream Frosting (see page 18).

4 Remove the cones from the refrigerator and set a cupcake inside each. Place in little milk jars or small glasses to serve.

SNOW PRINCESS PRESENTATION TRICK!

Tie ribbons around each milk jar or glass. Fill the bottom of each with Sixlets® candies to add color and give a little sweet treat to every special guest!

INGREDIENTS

....

1 pound of candy coating or Wilton Candy Melts® in assorted colors

12 packaged sugar ice cream cones

Pink, purple, and blue sprinkles

12 cupcakes of choice, Vanilla Cupcakes (page 34), Chia Chip Cupcakes (page 42), or your favorite cupcake flavor

Vanilla Buttercream Frosting (page 18)

MAKES 12 CUPCAKES

VANILLA BUTTERCREAM FROSTING

INGREDIENTS

....

3–3 1/2 cups powdered sugar

1/2 cup butter, softened

1 teaspoon pure vanilla extract

3–4 tablespoons whipping cream

1 Blend the sugar and butter with an electric mixer on low until well blended; then increase speed to medium and beat for another 3 minutes.

2 Add vanilla and 1 tablespoon whipping cream and continue to beat on medium for 1 minute, adding more cream if needed for spreading consistency.

**MAKES ENOUGH FOR
24 CUPCAKES,
A TWO-LAYER CAKE,
OR A 13x9-INCH SHEET PAN**

EATS
&
TREATS

WINTER WONDERLAND DIP

INGREDIENTS

....

2 tablespoons dried parsley

1 1/2 teaspoons dried dill weed

2 teaspoons garlic powder

2 teaspoons onion powder

2 teaspoons dried onion flakes

1/2 teaspoon ground white pepper

1 teaspoon dried chives

1 teaspoon sea salt

....

1 tablespoon Seasoning Mix

1/3 cup plain Greek yogurt*

1–2 teaspoons milk, your choice

Freshly chopped parsley or dill
(optional garnish)

SERVES 4

SEASONING MIX

1 Whisk the seasoning ingredients together until well blended. Place in a covered jar. Seasoning mix may be stored for up to 3 months.

DIP

1 To make Winter Wonderland Dip, combine the seasoning mix with Greek yogurt and milk, amounts depending on the consistency that you prefer.

2 Whisk to combine and top with optional fresh herb garnish. Store in the refrigerator for up to 1 week.

3 Serve with your favorite seasonal veggies, chips, or pretzels.

DF *Substitute with non-dairy yogurt for a dairy-free option.*

SAVORY SNOWBALL PASTA

1 Using snowflake cookie cutters, cut out 4 pieces of cheese and set aside until ready to use.

2 In a large mixing bowl, toss the pasta with parsley, basil, olive oil, salt, and pepper.

3 Divide pasta equally between 8–10 appetizer serving bowls and garnish with mozzarella balls and snowflake cheese cut-outs.

4 Serve at room temperature.

GF *Substitute with gluten-free pasta. Foodie Kids loves Bionaturae Gluten-Free Pastas. Check them out at: http://www.bionaturae.com/.*

INGREDIENTS

· · · · · · · · · · · · · · · · · ·

1-inch snowflakeshaped cookie cutters

4 slices mozzarella or provolone cheese

1 pound whole wheat pasta (penne, elbow, or any small pasta shape), cooked and drained*

1/4 cup fresh parsley, chopped

1/2 cup fresh basil, torn into bite-sized pieces

1/4 cup extra virgin olive oil

Sea salt and pepper to taste

1 cup small mozzarella balls

MAKES 8–10 BOWLS

MAGIC POWERS MINI PIZZAS

INGREDIENTS

· · · · · · · · · · · · · · · · ·

1 package yeast

2 tablespoons honey

1 cup warm water

1/8 teaspoon blue paste food coloring

1 teaspoon sea salt

3 tablespoons olive oil

1 1/2 cups white flour and 1 1/2 cups whole wheat flour, combined

1 5-inch, 1 2- to 3-inch, and 1 1- to 2-inch snowflake cookie cutter

12 slices of your favorite cheese or non-dairy cheese

Edible glitter

MAKES 8 PIZZAS

1 Combine the yeast, honey, and warm water, and let set for 5–10 minutes to allow yeast to "bloom."

2 Add blue food coloring, sea salt, and 1 tablespoon of olive oil to the yeast mixture; stir to combine.

3 Add flour 1/2 cup at a time, mixing well between each addition. Keep mixing and adding flour until the dough begins to pull away from the side of the bowl and a dough ball forms.

4 Drizzle an additional teaspoon or two of olive oil over the dough, rub the top of the surface, and cover with a cloth dish towel. Set in a warm place for 30–45 minutes to rise.

5 After the dough has risen, place it on a lightly floured work area and knead 2–3 minutes. Divide into 8 balls and flatten into round discs. Cut into a snowflake shape with the 5-inch cookie cutter.

6 Place on a prepared cookie sheet and bake for 5–8 minutes.

7 While the pizzas are baking, use a smaller, 2- to 3-inch snowflake cookie cutter to cut 8 slices of cheese into snowflakes. With the 1- to 2-inch snowflake cookie cutter, cut out 2 small snowflakes from each slice of the remaining 4 cheese slices for a total of 8 smaller snowflakes.

8 Remove pizza snowflakes from the oven and top with both the large and small cheese snowflakes. Dust pizzas with edible glitter and return to oven to bake an additional 3–5 minutes, or until cheese is very slightly melted. Remove from oven and serve warm, or at room temperature.

GF *Substitute with gluten-free flour, if desired.*

MAGIC SPELL MERINGUES

 DF GF Veg

INGREDIENTS

....

3 egg whites at room temperature*

3/4 cup sugar

1/4 teaspoon cream of tartar

1/2 teaspoon pure vanilla extract

MAKES 18–24 MERINGUES

1 Preheat oven to 250 degrees. Line two sheet pans with parchment paper.

2 In a large bowl, whip egg whites with an electric mixer until soft peaks form. With the mixer on, slowly add sugar, 1 tablespoon at a time. It's very important to add the sugar slowly or the egg whites will not whip up.

3 Add cream of tartar and vanilla extract. Continue beating until stiff peaks form.

4 Spoon or pipe mounds (about 2 tablespoons each) 1/2 inch apart onto prepared sheet pans.

5 Place both sheet pans on the middle rack of the preheated oven and bake for 1 hour.

6 Turn oven off, keep door closed, and allow meringues to stay in the oven for another 10 minutes.

7 Remove from oven and baking sheets. Store in a covered container for up to 3 days.

v ** Substitute 2 teaspoons of meringue powder and 2 tablespoons of water for each egg white for a vegan option.*

SNOW PRINCESS MERINGUE MADNESS!

- *Before baking the meringues, garnish with confetti sprinkles, mini chocolate chips, or baking size M&M's®.*

- *Dip the baked meringues into melted milk or white chocolate and garnish with chopped nuts, coconut, or sprinkles.*

- *You may also add food coloring to the egg whites to make pastel meringue cookies.*

SNOW PRINCESS CORONATION CAKE

1 Preheat oven to 350 degrees. Coat the round cake pans with cooking spray.

2 Prepare your cake mix and pour batter into each cake pan until they are half full. Any leftover cake batter may be used for cupcakes or for any use you desire. Tap each pan on the counter to eliminate air bubbles before placing in the oven.

3 Bake 30–35 minutes, watching for the smaller cakes to bake faster than the larger. Cakes should be lightly golden brown, and, when touched with your finger, should bounce back and not leave a fingerprint.

4 Remove from the oven and cool in their pans for 10–15 minutes on a cooling rack. Carefully remove each cake from its pan by placing a plate over the pan and inverting the cake onto the plate. Place the cakes on a wire rack for another 15 minutes before frosting.

INGREDIENTS

. . . .

2 6-inch and 2 8-inch round cake pans

Vanilla Cupcakes (page 34), tripled OR 3 packages cake mix, any flavor

Vanilla Buttercream Frosting (page 18)

Powdered sugar

1 package (2 pounds) white fondant

Blue paste food coloring

Assorted sizes and colors of sugar pearls and Sixlets®*

Tiara crown (optional adornment)

5 For the frosting, mix small amounts of blue paste food coloring into the Vanilla Buttercream Frosting from page 18 until you reach your desired color.

6 Stack and frost the two 8-inch layers, including an even layer of frosting in between.

7 For the fondant snow design, dust your work area with powdered sugar and roll out half of the fondant into one large round, about 16" in diameter. Create a scalloped design by cutting a curved, wavy edge around the perimeter. Place on top of the 8-inch layers and gently smooth down.

8 Stack and frost the two 6-inch layers like before. Carefully transfer onto the top of the 8-inch base. Roll and cut the remaining fondant into a second wavy round about 12" in diameter and place on top of smaller layer. Gently smooth down.

9 Adorn with a purchased tiara crown and decorate with Sixlets and sugar pearls.

* Sugar pearls are sold by Wilton and other cake decorating supplies companies.

MELTED SNOW DIP

WITH MAGIC FRUIT WANDS

1 To make Melted Snow Dip, combine all ingredients (besides fruit, skewers, and garnish) in a mixing bowl. Cover and refrigerate until ready to serve or up to 3 days.

2 To make the Magic Fruit Wands, place assorted fruits on wooden skewers.

3 Garnish dip with optional sprinkles or shredded coconut and serve with your Magic Fruit Wands.

(DF) (V) *Substitute with non-dairy soy, almond, or coconut yogurt, if desired.*

(GF) (Veg)

INGREDIENTS

· · · · · · · · · · · · · · · · ·

2 cups non-fat plain Greek yogurt*

1 teaspoon pure vanilla extract

1 tablespoon fresh orange juice

4–6 tablespoons pure maple syrup

1/4 teaspoon cinnamon

1/4 teaspoon freshly grated nutmeg

Assorted seasonal fresh fruits

6- to 8-inch wooden skewers

Rainbow confetti sprinkles or shredded coconut (optional garnish)

MAKES 2 CUPS OF DIP

SNOW-COVERED CUPCAKES

(VANILLA CUPCAKES)

INGREDIENTS

....

1 1/2 cups self-rising flour

1 1/4 cups all-purpose flour

1 cup unsalted butter, softened

2 cups sugar

4 large eggs at room temperature

1 cup milk, your choice

1 teaspoon pure vanilla extract

Vanilla Buttercream Frosting (page 18)

MAKES 24 CUPCAKES

1 Preheat oven to 350 degrees and line two 12-capacity muffin tins with cupcake papers; set aside until ready to use.

2 In a small bowl, combine flours; set aside.

3 In a large bowl, cream butter with an electric mixer on medium until smooth. Add the sugar gradually and beat until fluffy, about 3 minutes. Add the eggs, 1 at a time, beating well after each addition. Add the flour mixture in 3 parts, alternating with the milk and vanilla. With each addition, beat until the ingredients are incorporated, but do not overbeat. Using a rubber spatula, scrape down the batter in the bowl to make sure the ingredients are well blended.

4 Carefully spoon the batter into the cupcake liners, filling them about 3/4 full. Bake 20–25 minutes.

5 Cool the cupcakes in their tins for 15 minutes. Remove from the tins and let cool completely on a wire rack before frosting.

SWEET LITTLE SNOWBALL COOKIES

1 Preheat oven to 300 degrees. Line a cookie sheet with parchment paper; set aside until ready to use.

2 Melt butter in a large microwave-safe bowl. Add flour, sugar, salt, and vanilla extract, and mix until dough forms into a ball. Remove the dough from the bowl, and place on a lightly floured work area.

3 Form dough into 1-inch balls. Place them 1 inch apart on prepared cookie sheet, and bake 20–25 minutes, or until lightly golden.

4 Remove from the oven and let cool on cookie sheet for 10 minutes, and then transfer them to a wire rack.

5 Fill a bowl with powdered sugar and completely coat each ball with sugar and serve.

6 May be stored covered for up to one week.

Veg

INGREDIENTS

....

1 cup butter at room temperature

2 cups all-purpose flour

1/4 cup sugar

1/8 teaspoon salt

2 teaspoons pure vanilla extract

1/2 cup powdered sugar

MAKES 3 DOZEN COOKIES

SNOWFLAKE TORTILLA TREATS

1 Preheat oven to 350 degrees. Line sheet pans with parchment paper; set aside until ready to use.

2 Microwave tortillas for 10 seconds to warm; this will make them easier to cut.

3 Remove from the microwave and fold each tortilla in half and then in half again. With clean scissors, carefully snip shapes and make decorative cuts, just like you would to make a paper snowflake.

4 Place the tortilla snowflakes on prepared sheet pan and brush lightly with melted butter. Bake for 5–7 minutes or until edges are very lightly browned.

5 Remove the snowflakes from the oven and let cool 5 minutes before decorating.

6 Decorate with piping gel or icing by following the lines and shapes of the snowflakes. Sprinkle with sugars and shake gently to remove excess sugar.

INGREDIENTS

· · · · · · · · · · · · · ·

10 flour tortillas, any size*

1 tablespoon butter, melted

White piping gel or icing

Assorted colored crystal decorating sugars

MAKES 10 SNOWFLAKES

7 Allow the snowflakes to dry for 1 hour before serving. They are best served the day made.

 Substitute with gluten-free or corn tortillas, if desired.

ICICLE LOLLIPOPS

1 Preheat oven to 250 degrees. Line a sheet pan with parchment paper; set aside until ready to use.

2 Unwrap Jolly Ranchers. Lay 3–4 candies in a straight line, or 6 candies in a flower shape, on cookie sheet so that they are touching.

3 Bake for approximately 10 minutes; keep a close eye on them and remove them as soon as they start to melt but before they lose their shape.

4 Remove from the oven and sprinkle with optional glitter dust or sprinkles, and place the straw or lollipop stick into the center of each, turning them once to coat with the melted candy.

5 Allow lollipops to cool on the sheet pan for 10 minutes before removing.

6 Store flat and uncovered in a cool, dry place for up to 2 days.

INGREDIENTS

· · · · · · · · · · ·

Blue Jolly Ranchers®

Edible glitter dust and sprinkles (optional)

Assorted paper straws or lollipop sticks

MAKES 4–6 LOLLIPOPS, DEPENDING ON SIZE

ROYAL POPCORN CUPCAKES

(CHIA CHIP CUPCAKES)

1 Preheat oven to 350 degrees and line a 12-capacity muffin tin with paper liners; set aside until ready to use.

2 Mix water with 1 tablespoon of chia seeds. Let stand for 5 minutes until it forms a gel.

3 Whisk together coconut flour, coconut palm sugar, and the remaining 1 tablespoon of chia seeds in a large bowl. Add eggs, coconut oil, vanilla extract, and chia seed gel. Mix well to combine ingredients. Stir in chocolate chips.

4 Pour mixture evenly into prepared muffin tin and bake 20–25 minutes. Remove from the oven and cool on a wire rack for 5 minutes before removing from tin.

5 Frost with Vanilla Buttercream Frosting (page 18).

INGREDIENTS

....

1/4 cup water

2 tablespoons chia seeds

1/2 cup all-purpose flour

1/2 cup granulated sugar

2 eggs at room temperature

1/2 cup coconut oil

1 tablespoon pure vanilla extract

1/2 cup milk chocolate chips

Vanilla Buttercream Frosting (page 18)

Freshly popped popcorn

Candy coating (optional)

MAKES 12 CUPCAKES

6 Decorate with plenty of freshly popped organic popcorn.

DO YOU WANT TO BAKE-A-SNOWMAN?

1 In a large bowl, combine butter, brown sugar, egg, and molasses with an electric mixer. Add dry ingredients and mix completely. Remove the dough from the bowl and shape into a flat disc. Cover with plastic wrap and chill 2–3 hours or overnight.

2 Remove dough from the refrigerator and let sit 10 minutes before cutting out into cookies.

3 Preheat oven to 350 degrees. Line 2 cookie sheets with parchment paper and lightly coat with cooking spray; set aside until ready to use.

4 Dust work area with flour and roll out dough to approximately 1/4- to 1/2-inch thickness. Cut out cookies. Place a wooden craft stick into each cookie, pressing down lightly to adhere. Bake for 10–12 minutes. Remove from the oven and place the cookie sheet on a wire rack for 5 minutes.

5 Remove cookies from the cookie sheet and let cool.

INGREDIENTS

. . . .

3/4 cup butter, softened

1/2 cup brown sugar, packed

1 egg

3/4 cup molasses

3 cups all-purpose flour*

1/4 teaspoon salt

2 teaspoons powdered ginger

1 teaspoon cinnamon

1/2 teaspoon cloves

1/2 teaspoon nutmeg

6-inch wooden craft sticks (one per cookie)

GF *Substitute with gluten-free flour, if desired.*

**MAKES 8–10
4-INCH SNOWMEN**

DECORATIONS

············

1 Lightly dust work area with powdered sugar and roll out white fondant. Cut and shape into 3 lopsided circles of various sizes to create the snowman's head, chest, and tummy. White fondant may also be used to create a tooth for the snowman; set aside until ready to use.

Colored fondants (white, orange, turquoise, brown, and black, or your choice of colors)

Sugar eyes

Small, white marshmallows

White frosting

Q-Tips or small, clean paintbrushes

2 Create the nose with tiny bits of orange fondant. Shape arms, fingers, hair, and eyebrows with brown fondant by rolling into tiny "worms" to fit each face. Form the mouth with small bits of black fondant. Make the buttons by forming assorted colors of fondants into tiny balls.

3 Use small dots of white frosting to adhere the body, sugar eyes, and marshmallow feet onto each snowman.

4 Use a tiny bit of water on a Q-tip or small paint brush to adhere facial features and all other decorations to the white fondant.

SNOW PRINCESS KITCHEN TRIVIA: *Fondant is sweet candy dough that is made in many colors. Pastry chefs use it to decorate cakes, cupcakes, and cookies, and it feels just like Play-Doh®!*

MUFFINS-IN-A-JAR

1 Preheat oven to 375 degrees. Generously coat the insides of mason jars with cooking spray. Place on a cookie sheet; set aside until ready to use.

2 In a large bowl, cream butter and sugar with an electric mixer. Add egg, vanilla, and milk. Mix well.

3 Add flour, baking powder, and salt; mix to combine.

4 Carefully fold in blueberries with a rubber spatula. Spoon batter evenly between the jars.

5 Bake for about 15–20 minutes, until tops are golden and a toothpick inserted in the center comes out clean.

6 Remove from the oven and cool 10 minutes before serving, since the jar will be too hot. Serve warm or at room temperature.

INGREDIENTS

. . . .

Mason jars (4 ounces each)

1/4 cup butter, softened

1/4 cup sugar

1 large egg

1 teaspoon pure vanilla extract

1/4 cup milk, your choice

1 cup all-purpose flour

1 1/2 teaspoons baking powder

1/4 teaspoon salt

1 cup fresh or frozen blueberries

MAKES 10–12 MUFFINS

HOSTESS IDEA: *Tie a pretty ribbon around each jar before serving and send the jar (and lid) home with each friend at your party. These little jars are great for keeping all sorts of secret princess treasures and trinkets!*

HER MAJESTY'S ROYAL TEACUP-CAKES

INGREDIENTS

....

18 china or pottery teacups* or small mugs

Vanilla Cupcake recipe (page 34) with the addition of 1/3 cup rainbow-colored sprinkles

Vanilla candy coating

Snowflake candy molds

Small pretzel sticks

Vanilla Buttercream Frosting (page 18)

Paste food coloring, purple and blue

Tiny decorative ribbons

Snowflake sprinkles

Small sugar pearls

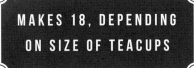

MAKES 18, DEPENDING ON SIZE OF TEACUPS

1 Preheat oven to 350 degrees. Spray all teacups or mugs generously with cooking spray; set aside until ready to use.

2 Make cupcakes according to the Vanilla Cupcake recipe, stirring in the sprinkles after the batter has been mixed completely.

3 Divide batter evenly between teacups and place on a cookie sheet.

4 Bake 25–30 minutes and remove from oven to cool before frosting and decorating.

5 While cupcakes are baking, melt candy coating according to package directions and fill 18 small snowflake candy molds. Place 1 small pretzel stick onto each mold. Allow to cool and harden at room temperature for 30 minutes, or place in the fridge for 15 minutes.

6 While candy coating is hardening, divide frosting into two bowls; color half with

purple food coloring and the other half with blue food coloring. Frost cupcakes while candy snowflakes harden.

7 When candy snowflakes have hardened, remove from molds and tie a little ribbon onto each. Place on top of frosted cupcakes and decorate with sprinkles and sugar pearls.

* Not all teacups can survive the heat of baking, so don't use an heirloom set. Dishwasher-safe teacups are your best bet. Look for microwave or oven safe products.

SIPPING TREATS

ICE PRINCESS PUNCH

1 Combine Gatorade® and sparkling water in a large punch bowl; stir together.

2 Add marshmallows right before serving.

* Use 1 or 2 liters of sparkling water, depending on how fizzy you want the punch to be. If fizz is not for you, leave it out and increase the amount of Gatorade® needed to serve your guests.

SERVES 15–18

WARM HUGS SNOW CUPS

INGREDIENTS

....

6 cups milk, your choice

1/4 cup granulated or coconut sugar

3 teaspoons pure vanilla extract

1/2 teaspoon ground cinnamon

1/4 teaspoon ground ginger

1/8 teaspoon ground cardamom

Mini marshmallows and peppermints (optional garnish)

SERVES 12

1 Combine milk and sugar in a large saucepan over low heat until warm, being careful not to boil. Remove from heat and stir in vanilla extract and spices.

2 Divide evenly between cups, top with optional marshmallow and peppermint garnish, and serve warm.

ENCHANTED PERFECT PINK LEMONADE

1 Combine warm water and sugar in a large bowl.

2 Add lemon juice and grenadine syrup.

3 Chill for 2 hours prior to serving.

4 Add optional ice and serve in your favorite container and punch cups.

SNOW PRINCESS MAGICAL DECORATING AND SERVING IDEAS:

- *Make up an extra batch of lemonade and freeze in ice trays to make lemonade ice cubes to use instead of regular ice cubes.*

- *Turn any plain cup or glass into a "Sugar Sipper Cup"; just dampen the drinking rim of the cup or glass with the juice from a lime, lemon, or orange. Pour about 1/4 cup of colored sugar onto a small plate. Dip the dampened rim of the drinking cup into the sugar and Voila! a Sugar Sipper Cup!*

INGREDIENTS

....

6 cups warm water

1/2–1 cup of sugar

6–7 lemons, juiced (about 1 1/2 cups juice)

1–2 tablespoons grenadine syrup

Ice (optional)

SERVES 12

SNOW QUEEN COOLERS

1 In a blender, combine the milk and grape juice concentrate. Add ice cream or frozen yogurt and blend until smooth. Serve immediately.

SNOW PRINCESS SNOWFLAKE TREAT: *Use white fondant to create a mini snowflake to garnish and decorate your drink. Roll out fondant and cut with a small snowflake cookie cutter. Insert a small toothpick and allow it to dry uncovered for 12–24 hours (fondant will harden as it dries).*

Serve with any drink or place on top of a cupcake for a Snow Princess treat!

INGREDIENTS

· · · · · · · · · · · · · · ·

1 cup milk, your choice

3/4 cup grape juice concentrate, thawed

2 cups vanilla ice cream or frozen yogurt, softened

SERVES 4

FROZEN HOT CHOCOLATE

WITH MARSHMALLOW SNOWMEN

INGREDIENTS

....

2 cups milk, your choice

5 packets (1.25 ounces each) of your favorite hot chocolate mix

1 teaspoon pure vanilla extract

4 cups crushed ice

Whipped cream* (optional)

1/4 cup mini chocolate chips, mint chocolate chips, or shaved chocolate (optional)

....

White candy coating, 2 tablespoons (or one square) per snowman

Large marshmallows, 3 per snowman

Mini marshmallows, 2 per snowman

Black and orange fondants

Sugar eyes

SERVES 4

FROZEN HOT CHOCOLATE

1 Place milk, hot chocolate packets, and vanilla extract in a large bowl and mix with a whisk until combined and frothy. Add crushed ice to 4 clear cups or glasses and pour in chocolate mix, dividing evenly.

2 Stir well and garnish with optional whipped cream and chocolate.

MARSHMALLOW SNOWMEN

1 Melt 1/2 cup of candy coating according to package directions; set aside until ready to use and cover and to keep warm by leaving it in the microwave or on the stovetop.

2 Decorate 1 large marshmallow with a face using black fondant to create

eyebrows, mouth, and hair. Attach sugar eyes to the marshmallow with a tiny bit of melted candy coating; set aside until ready to use.

3 Create 2 black fondant arms and insert into second marshmallow. Add 2 black fondant buttons with a tiny bit of candy coating to the center of second marshmallow.

4 Flatten the last marshmallow with a rolling pin; set aside.

5 Assemble each snowman by using candy coating to "glue" together each section. First, glue the 2 mini marshmallows to the flattened marshmallow for feet. Next, glue the marshmallow with arms to the flattened marshmallow. Finally, glue the head portion of the marshmallow to the top of the marshmallow with arms.

6 Allow the snowman to harden and dry for at least 30 minutes before serving.

7 To make ahead, completely dry for 30 minutes; cover and store in freezer for up to 3 months. Do not thaw before garnishing.

PARTY CRAFTS

SPARKLING SNOW PLAY DOUGH

INGREDIENTS

3 cups flour

1 1/2 cups salt

2 tablespoons cream of tartar

3 cups water

3 tablespoons vegetable oil

1/2 teaspoon clear peppermint extract

1/2 cup white or sliver sequins combined with 2 tablespoons silver or blue craft glitter

1 Combine the flour, salt, and cream of tartar in a large saucepan. Add water, oil, and peppermint extract. Cook over low heat, stirring constantly. After about 5 minutes it will start to pull away from the sides of the pan and form a dough ball.

2 Remove pan from heat and turn out dough onto a work surface covered with the sequins and glitter. Knead until combined and cooled.

3 Sprinkle with additional glitter if desired. Store tightly covered for up to 2 weeks.

MAKES ABOUT 6 CUPS

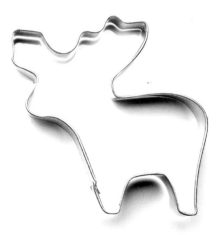

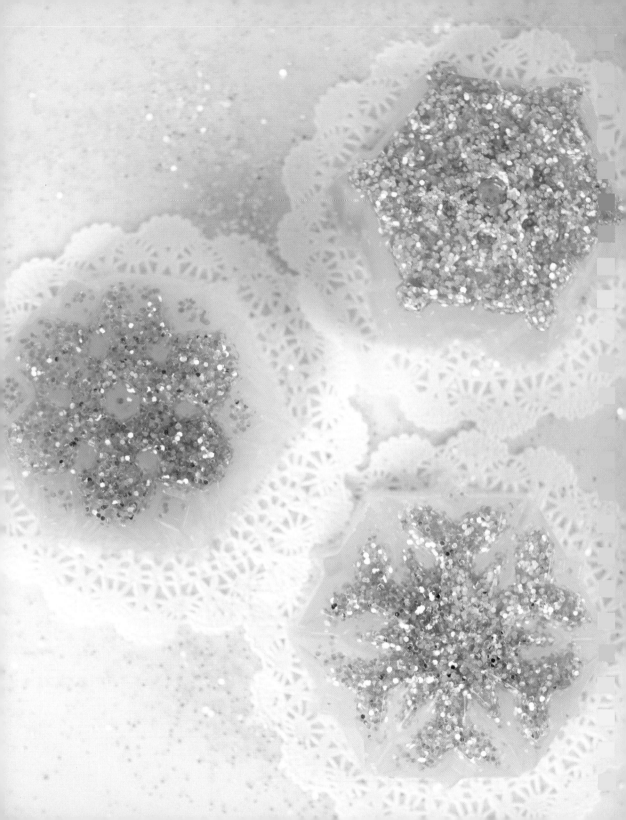

TWINKLING SNOWFLAKE SOAPS

1 Spray snowflake cupcake or candy molds with cooking spray. Place assorted toys into each mold face down.

2 Combine glycerin soap with scented oil and pour equally into each mold. Set aside to harden for 1 hour.

3 Remove from mold and wrap in cellophane; tie with a ribbon for a perfect party favor.

* 1 pound fills approximately 10–12 2-inch molds.

INGREDIENTS

. . . .

Snowflake cupcake or candy molds

Small plastic toys, rings, mini erasers, etc.

1 pound* glycerin soap, melted

4–6 drops scented oil, your fragrance choice

CRYSTAL POWER CANDY NECKLACES

INGREDIENTS

....

Assorted colors of rock candy on strings

Narrow satin ribbons, 2 feet per necklace

1 Tie rock candy to satin ribbon and secure ends together to tie around child's neck.

GLIMMERING ICE GLITTER LOTION

1 Combine lotion and aloe vera gel in a small bowl.

2 Stir in scented oil and glitter.

3 Spoon mixture into a small container with label.

4 Store up to one month.

INGREDIENTS

....

1/2 cup non-scented or lightly scented lotion

1/2 cup clear aloe vera gel

3–5 drops scented oil

1 teaspoon blue or silver craft glitter

MAKES 1 CUP

LET IT GLOW MELTED SNOW

INGREDIENTS

1/4 cup Elmer's® Glue

1/4 cup warm water

Paste food coloring, any color

1 tablespoon glow-in-the-dark paint

2 tablespoons warm water

1/4 teaspoon borax

1 Combine glue, water, and food coloring in a small bowl. Add glow-in-the-dark paint and mix well.

2 In a separate cup, mix warm water with borax.

3 Pour the borax water into the glue mixture, stir with a Popsicle® stick or spoon, and watch the magic happen.

Store in the refrigerator in an airtight container for up to one week.

"DO THE MAGIC" BUBBLES AND WANDS

BUBBLES

1 Mix all ingredients together in container with a lid (small wide mouth Mason jars work well). Shake well and let set overnight before using.

WANDS

1 Cut wire approximately 12 inches long so you have enough room to create the decorative bubble-blowing end of the wand.

2 Make the decorative wand by shaping the wire around a small cookie cutter, leaving approximately 6 inches for the handle.

3 Place beads on the remaining wire and allow about 1/2 inch of unadorned wire at the end to form a small circle, which will allow children to hold the bubble wand easily.

4 Tie on ribbons and "do the magic"!

INGREDIENTS

....

1 cup water

3 tablespoons liquid dishwashing detergent (Blue Dawn® Ultra is what we use)

1 tablespoon liquid glycerin

1/2 teaspoon sugar

....

Craft wire

Small snowflake or star cookie cutter

Assorted craft beads

Ribbons

CONVERSIONS

Volume Measurements

U.S.	METRIC
1 teaspoon	5 ml
1 tablespoon	15 ml
1/4 cup	60 ml
1/3 cup	75 ml
1/2 cup	125 ml
2/3 cup	150 ml
3/4 cup	175 ml
1 cup	250 ml

Weight Measurements

U.S.	METRIC
1/2 ounce	15 g
1 ounce	30 g
3 ounces	90g
4 ounces	115 g
8 ounces	225 g
12 ounces	350 g
1 pound	450 g
2 1/4 pounds	1 kg

Temperature Conversion

FAHRENHEIT	CELSIUS
250	120
300	150
325	160
350	180
375	190
400	200
425	220
450	230

MEET BARBARA

Barbara Beery, the bestselling author of *The Pink Princess Cookbook*, has been a spokesperson for such national companies as Sun-Maid Raisin, Uncle Ben's, Borden's, Kellogg's Rice Krispies, and Step 2. Barbara has been a contributing writer to *FamilyFun*, the country's leading family magazine. She has appeared twice on the *Today Show* and the CBN with Pat Robertson. Beery's business has been featured in the *New York Times* and *Entrepreneur* magazine, as well as dozens of other local and national publications. She has worked closely with Get Moving, Cookies for Kids Cancer, Rachael Ray's Yum-o! Organization, and No Kids Hungry.

Barbara is the author of 12 books, having sold more than 500,000 copies. She resides in Austin, Texas.

ABOUT FOODIE KIDS

Foodie Kids cooking school, retail store, and a drop-in make-your-own snack counter, The Makery®, is the largest and most unique kids culinary center in the country.

The beginning started in Barbara's home kitchen twenty-five years ago teaching cooking classes. Through the years the small, home-based cooking school grew into an operation that was no longer manageable to operate from her home. With years of hard work, the small cottage business turned into a retail culinary destination for kids and families to celebrate birthdays, take cooking classes, host field trips, and enjoy summer cooking camps.

For more information, visit www.foodie-kids.com.

ABOUT FAMILIUS

Welcome to a place where mothers are celebrated, not compared. Where heart is at the center of our families, and family at the center of our homes. Where boo boos are still kissed, cake beaters are still licked, and mistakes are still okay. Welcome to a place where books—and family—are beautiful. Familius: a book publisher dedicated to helping families be happy.

VISIT OUR WEBSITE: WWW.FAMILIUS.COM

Our website is a different kind of place. Get inspired, read articles, discover books, watch videos, connect with our family experts, download books and apps and audiobooks, and along the way, discover how values and happy family life go together.

JOIN OUR FAMILY

There are lots of ways to connect with us! Subscribe to our newsletters at www.familius.com to receive uplifting daily inspiration, essays from our Pater Familius, a free ebook every month, and the first word on special discounts and Familius news.

GET BULK DISCOUNTS

If you feel a few friends and family might benefit from what you've read, let us know and we'll be happy to provide you with quantity discounts. Simply email us at specialorders@familius.com.

Website: www.familius.com
Facebook: www.facebook.com/paterfamilius
Twitter: @familiustalk, @paterfamilius1
Pinterest: www.pinterest.com/familius

FAMILIUS